GW00502503

Samuel French -
New York—Hollywood — Toronto

3013020971309 7

CHARACTERS

Lucile
Baptiste, her maid
Gabrielle, another maid
Edouard
Madame, Lucile's mother

THE MUSIC LOVERS

An elegant drawing-room in a Paris apartment. Double doors in the centre open into the vestibule where one can see the front door, which opens onto a landing. The furniture is heavy. There is a round table with several chairs, a sofa etc. Other furniture is dotted about. DS *left is a piano, either baby grand or upright*

Baptiste, the maid in her mid-twenties, is dusting ornaments on an occasional table. Lucile, just twenty, naïve and pretty despite a certain dowdiness enforced by her mother, is practising scales on the piano. Baptiste breaks off from her not very serious task to admire Lucile

Baptiste (*clapping*) Bravo! Bravo...! Oh, pardon, mademoiselle, I forgot myself. But I do love the way you rush up and down like that. Just like the wind!

Lucile Baptiste, what are you talking about? What wind?

Baptiste Your wind, mademoiselle. I mean your playing is like the wind.

Lucile That is not wind, Baptiste. Those are my scales.

Baptiste Well, I like to think of it as wind. It's more imaginative. It reminds me of when I was a little girl in the country. We used to get wind like that all the time. (*She makes a blowing sound to imitate the wind in the country*)

Lucile I am happy to say we don't get wind like that here in Paris.

Baptiste More's the pity, mademoiselle Lucile. Everything so sophisticated. I don't know what this place is coming to. Did you know, the apartment downstairs——

Lucile I don't want to hear any of your gossip, Baptiste. Has Mother gone out?

Baptiste A quarter of an hour ago.

Lucile Poor Mama! It's such a bore for her.

Baptiste Why, what happened?

Lucile Didn't you know? She's been summonsed.

Baptiste Poor madame! What's "summonsed"?

Lucile To appear in court. The charge is one of public indecency.

Baptiste Your mother indecent in public, whatever next!

Lucile Not her, Baptiste! She's been summonsed as a witness. It all happened just outside here. A woman hit a policeman and insulted a coachman, or it may have been the other way round...

Baptiste I don't call that indecent. Unwise possibly...

Lucile Never mind about that now. I haven't got time to gossip. I need to practice.

She applies herself to the scales for a while, but becomes conscious of Baptiste staring at her

(*Pointedly*) You like the piano, do you?

Baptiste Oh, yes! When it's mademoiselle playing. Not when I am.

Lucile You never told me you knew the piano.

Baptiste Oh, yes, mademoiselle, but not to play, if you follow me.

Lucile I can't say I do.

Baptiste We had an old one at home in the country.

Lucile And you used it?

Baptiste To keep the butter in. It would have been a waste just to use it to play tunes on.

Lucile In Paris, Baptiste, we are less resourceful with our furniture. (*She starts her scales again*) Oh, that reminds me. I am expecting a gentleman.

Baptiste Mademoiselle! And after all that your mother said——

Lucile It's quite all right, Baptiste. My mother knows all about it.

Baptiste And she approves?

Lucile She arranged it herself.

Baptiste Never!

Lucile He's not that sort of gentleman, Baptiste. He's a professor of music. He's come to teach me the piano.

Baptiste (*disappointed*) Oh.

Lucile He's really quite famous. Mother says. He's what they call "*un maestro di primo cartello.*"

Baptiste You'll have to translate, mademoiselle. I don't know English.

Lucile I've never met him. Mother made all the arrangements. I'm afraid I can't even remember his name, but it's very well known.

Baptiste (*helpfully*) Molière, mademoiselle?

Lucile No, of course not Molière! I'd know if it was Molière. Anyway, Molière's dead.

Baptiste Famous people usually are.

Lucile Not this one. If I could remember his name I'd recognize it. Anyway, this famous professor should be arriving any minute now. He'll come to the door and ask for madame.

Baptiste And I'll tell him that madame's out.

Lucile Certainly not! You let him in. He's come to see me.

Baptiste But madame said——

Lucile I know what madame said, but she can't possibly object to a music professor she's hired herself. He's probably about eighty anyway.

Baptiste I've known men of eighty who——

Lucile This professor whatever-his-name-is isn't just any old teacher, he's a maestro. You can't have him running about like a... like a...

Baptiste Like a servant.

Lucile You can't keep them waiting; they keep you waiting. So you're to let him in. Understood?

Baptiste Yes, mademoiselle.

Lucile Now I must go and tidy myself up. This is my first day. I want to make a good impression with the maestro.

Baptiste But you said he was eighty.

Lucile I said he was *probably* eighty, Baptiste. One has to prepare for every possibility.

Lucile exits right

Baptiste continues dusting

Gabrielle, another maid, but much smarter and more sophisticated than Baptiste, pokes her head round the door

Gabrielle (*hissing*) Baptiste! Baptiste!

Baptiste Gabrielle! What are you doing here? How did you get in?

Gabrielle Me, I've got a key to all the apartments here. Your mistress out?

Baptiste Madame's out. Mademoiselle's in there. What about yours?

Gabrielle My mademoiselle? You'll never believe this. She's in court.

Baptiste No! Mademoiselle Dubarroy in court! What for?

Gabrielle Indecency. She insulted a policeman and hit a coachman; or it may have been the other way round.

Baptiste What a coincidence! My madame——

Gabrielle It happened just outside here. You see she came home from the theatre a little overtired... and perhaps she'd dined at *Maxim*'s a little too well——

Baptiste But this is extraordinary! You see my madame is going to be a witness at the trial.

Gabrielle Oh, lor! This is dreadful!

Baptiste Why?

Gabrielle Because your madame hates my mademoiselle. She thinks she's immoral.

Baptiste No!

Gabrielle And she's not immoral at all. She's just... high-spirited. And your madame is always complaining if there's any noise from our apartment down below. It's true my lady works late, but that's the theatre for you. In the theatre you often don't stop working even when you go to bed.

Baptiste So I've heard.

Gabrielle It's the lines you have to learn, you see. My mademoiselle can often be up all night learning, if she's been given a difficult part.

Baptiste I never knew that.

Gabrielle It's a fact. Anyhow, I came up here because we're in trouble and I thought you might help us out. You see, my lady has an admirer.

Baptiste Only one?

Gabrielle This is a special one. He comes from the provinces and he's immensely rich. In fact they've never set eyes on each other.

Baptiste How did it start?

Gabrielle This man—I forget his name—just wrote to her out of the blue. She's very famous you see.

Baptiste Ah. Like a maestro.

Gabrielle Well, they arranged to meet for the first time at her apartment today. Only suddenly this court case comes up. Well, my lady doesn't want the gentleman to know she's in court. These people from the provinces can be very strait-laced, you know.

Baptiste Is that so?

Gabrielle It's a fact. And it wouldn't be good if my lady is out when he arrives for their first rendezvous. So I had a wonderful idea.

Baptiste Tell me.

Gabrielle It's very simple. I told the concierge to send the gentleman up to the apartment above ours—this one—by mistake.

Baptiste I'm not following you.

Gabrielle Simple. The concierge sends the gentleman here by mistake on purpose.

Baptiste Why?

Gabrielle Because I've told him to.

Baptiste Then it wouldn't be a mistake, would it? Unless he sent him to your apartment accidentally instead of deliberately by mistake here.

Gabrielle Stop confusing things, Baptiste! The gentleman arrives here. Understood?

Baptiste I don't think——

Gabrielle And all you have to do is keep him here until my mistress is back from the court. Then when she does come back, you say "Oh dear, monsieur, you must have come to the wrong apartment; if it's Mademoiselle Dubarroy you want, she's down below." You see! Simple!

Baptiste And how do I know when your lady is back?

Gabrielle Easy. I give you a signal. I come up here to give you back your feather duster. (*Taking her duster*) And I say, "Thank you for lending me this. It came in very handy."

Baptiste It all sounds far too difficult.

Gabrielle Only because I've worked it out so carefully.

Baptiste But your lady might be ages. You know what these courts are like.

Gabrielle I do not. Neither does mademoiselle.

Baptiste But how do I keep this gentleman up here all that time?

Gabrielle It won't be long. You will do this for me, won't you, Baptiste? If you do I promise you tickets to see my mademoiselle in her show, "Low-Life Lola."

Baptiste Well, I don't know...

Gabrielle Oh, thank you, Baptiste! I knew you would!

Baptiste No! Impossible!

Gabrielle Why not?

Baptiste Because my mademoiselle is expecting a gentleman.

Gabrielle Never!

Baptiste No! It's not like that. He's a musician.

Gabrielle That's no guarantee of purity. My lady has terrible trouble at the theatre with her first violin.

Baptiste This one's a music professor and he's teaching her the piano.

Gabrielle I'll tell the concierge to send him away.

Baptiste You can't do that! Besides, we don't know what he looks like.

Gabrielle I'll tell the concierge to send anyone who looks musical away. (*Holding up the duster*) Remember: "Thank you for lending me this. It came in very handy."

She exits rapidly

Baptiste But I didn't. Wait!

Lucile (*off*) Baptiste!

Baptiste (*starting to go*) Just a moment, mademoiselle. I have to——

Lucile enters. She has improved her appearance considerably for the arrival of the music teacher. Perhaps she has rather overdone it, but she is only twenty

Lucile Baptiste! Where are you going? Who was that?

Baptiste Nowhere. Nobody.

Lucile What have you done with your duster?

Baptiste Nothing.

Lucile What do you mean, nothing?

Baptiste Oh, mademoiselle, you have made yourself look nice.

Lucile Do you think so? Really? You don't think I've overdone it?

Baptiste Well, mademoiselle, don't you think he'll be more interested what you sound like, rather than what you look like? Now, if you'll excuse me, I really must— (*she starts to go off* c)

Lucile Baptiste! Come back here! Where are you going?

Baptiste Nowhere, mademoiselle.

Lucile Then you can go and tidy up my bedroom.

Baptiste Very good, mademoiselle.

Lucile And when the bell rings, you must answer the door.

Baptiste But, mademoiselle, he may be... he may not be...

Lucile What?

Baptiste Nothing, mademoiselle.

Lucile Then do as you are told.

Baptiste But——

Lucile Baptiste! You don't want me to tell madame about you.

Baptiste No, mademoiselle. But——

Lucile Go!

Baptiste exits

Lucile sits at the piano

Poor Baptiste! Still knows nothing about how we do things in
Paris. (*She starts to play scales*) Do re me fa sol la si do, do si
la sol fa mi re do re me—Ouf! What a bore! Mother says that
nowadays you can't get married unless you know how to play
the piano. I suppose she's right. She's always right. "Unless
you can do your scales properly, you'll never get a husband."
I don't know. I suppose it keeps the fingers supple. But I can't
believe that you won't make a good wife unless you have
supple fingers. It doesn't make sense. I'm going to speak my
mind. If a man came along who wanted to marry me, I'd be
quite straightforward, I'd say,"Monsieur, here I am, twenty
years of age, I'm not awfully good at the piano; but I don't
expect you to be superb on the flute. Marriage isn't about
making music the whole time. It may be a duet, but it can be
played on other instruments. Such as... Well, I mean..." I'd say,
"If you want to marry me without piano, as I am, here's my
hand. But if it's music you're after, well, good afternoon and I
hope it keeps fine for you." There! (*She plays a decisive chord
and shuts the lid of the piano. Then wearily she opens it again*)
Oh dear! I don't want to upset Mother. The sacrifices we girls
have to make!

The bell rings

Baptiste!

Baptiste enters from the bedroom

Baptiste Yes, mademoiselle.
Lucile Answer the door, Baptiste. It's the maestro.
Baptiste Mademoiselle, I'm not sure if——
Lucile Show him in, Baptiste. I'm just going into the bedroom

to...

Baptiste But, mademoiselle, you've been in there already.

Lucile There's some music in there which I've forgotten. Answer the door, Baptiste.

Lucile exits into the bedroom

Baptiste I wonder who this is—the masher or the maestro!

The bell rings again

Lucile (*from the bedroom*) Answer the door, Baptiste!

Baptiste (*going*) Please, God, let him be eighty!

She goes through the double doors and into the vestibule

We see her opening the front door of the apartment to Edouard, a flashily dressed, amiable-looking young man. He is from the provinces and by no means as self-assured as he first appears to be

Edouard I say, have I come to the right place? Your concierge seemed not too sure about it.

Baptiste If monsieur will step this way. Mademoiselle is in the bedroom, but she'll be with you in a moment.

Edouard (*following Baptiste into the room*) I have come to the right place. (*Pulling out a rather over-large visiting card and handing it to Baptiste*) You recognize the name?

Baptiste (*barely glancing at the card*) Oh, yes. (*Hopefully*) It's very famous, isn't it?

Edouard (*laughing*) Famous! That's a good one!

Baptiste (*reading the card*) Monsieur Edouard Lorillot. (*Aside*) Peculiar name! Are you sure it isn't Professor Lorillot?

Edouard (*laughing*) Professor! That's a good one!

Baptiste (*aside*) I was afraid of that.

Edouard I'm from Toulouse, you know.

Baptiste Really, monsieur?

Edouard But I was brought up in Dunkirk.

Baptiste That would explain a great deal, monsieur.

Edouard And I'm a millionaire! Well, I have fifteen thousand a year. In Toulouse that counts as being a millionaire. I have lots of friends. They say I'm more Parisian than the Parisians.

Baptiste That wouldn't surprise me at all, monsieur.

Edouard I go to the best tailor, the best hairdresser. I'm on nodding terms with a prince. I go riding with a duke. I often lend him my best horse. Only one thing missing. I expect you can guess what that is.

Baptiste Monsieur?

Edouard An affair. But not just any old affair. Something a bit smart. I mean, if you're going to do it, you might as well go for the best, eh?

Baptiste Oh, yes.

Edouard And the Dubarroy. She's the tops, isn't she?

Baptiste (*nodding and looking towards the front door*) Mmm!

Edouard I mean, where your mademoiselle is concerned, chic just isn't the word!

Baptiste No, it isn't!

Edouard Look at this place for instance! Chic! That's what I'd call it. Everything about it, chic! (*Going to the bedroom door,* R) And this door! Chic!

Baptiste Don't go in there! That's the bedroom.

Edouard That's for later, eh? Chic!

Baptiste (*unable to take this any longer*) Monsieur, I must tell you——

Lucile enters with some music under her arm. She has beautified herself even more and this time has definitely overdone it, but Edouard is evidently much taken with the effect

Lucile Please forgive me for keeping you waiting, monsieur, but I couldn't find my music.

Edouard Couldn't find your...? That's quite all right, mademoiselle. Quite all right!

Baptiste Mademoiselle——

Lucile Baptiste, will you go and tidy up the bedroom, please.

Baptiste But I tidied it up just now, mademoiselle.

Lucile Well, it's untidy again. Go on with you.

Edouard gooses Baptiste as she goes past

Edouard That's right, you go and tidy up the bedroom. Chic!

Lucile gives him a look of astonishment

Pardon, mademoiselle.

Baptiste gives them a despairing look and exits to the bedroom

There is an awkward pause

Lucile I'm so sorry, please excuse me, but I've forgotten your name.

Edouard (*handing her another of his cards*) Lorillot. Edouard Lorillot.

Lucile Lorillot. Of course! How silly of me. (*Aside*) Peculiar name!

Edouard I'm not likely to forget *your* name.

Lucile No? (*Sensing a compliment*) You're too kind, monsieur!

Edouard If I may say so, mademoiselle, your photographs don't do you justice.

Lucile (*startled*) My photographs!
Edouard They make you look much older somehow.
Lucile You've seen photographs of me?
Edouard Naturally, mademoiselle.
Lucile Ah. I suppose my mother showed them to you.
Edouard (*laughing*) Mother! That's a good one.

Lucile stares at him in astonishment. There is an awkward pause

Lucile Please sit down, monsieur.
Edouard (*sitting on the sofa*) Here?
Lucile If you like.
Edouard Very chic!

*He pats the place next to him on the sofa. Lucile does not respond.
An awkward pause. They smile shyly at each other*

Lucile (*indicating the music she is holding*) I never go anywhere
   without my music.
Edouard Oh, yes. There's nothing like music, is there...?
Lucile Nothing. It's beautiful, isn't it?
Edouard What?
Lucile Music.
Edouard (*anxious to please*) Absolutely. I adore it.
Lucile (*likewise*) So do I. Completely... Of course, it is hard
   going when you're a beginner.
Edouard Is it? Well, I wouldn't know.
Lucile You mean you always found it easy?
Edouard What?
Lucile (*aside*) He's a bit conceited, but I suppose all great artists
   are. Are you fond of Wagner, monsieur?
Edouard Wagner? You mean the chemist?
Lucile The chemist?

Edouard The chemist in Toulouse. Adolphe Wagner. You know him?

Lucile No! The composer.

Edouard Oh, the composer Wagner. Yes, of course.

Lucile You like him?

Edouard I've heard people talking about him. Yes, it's Wagner this, Wagner that the whole time, isn't it? Now then, mademoiselle, shall we discuss something a little more... how shall I say...?

Lucile And Mozart? What do you think about Mozart?

Edouard Eh...? I can't say I do much. Never really got round to it.

Lucile Well then, who is your favourite composer, monsieur?

Edouard Mmm? Oh well... I suppose it must be... Cordillard.

Lucile I've never heard of Cordillard.

Edouard (*boasting*) He's a friend of mine, you know, as a matter of fact.

Lucile Ah!

Edouard Amazingly clever. Do you know "My Chick from Chicago"?

Lucile I'm afraid not.

Edouard He wrote that.

Lucile Did he?

Edouard Catchy little number. (*He starts to sing it, then perhaps gets up and executes a few dance steps by way of accompaniment*)

> You are my chick from Chicago!
> Chick from Chicago!
> Chick from Chicago!
> You're such a chic little chick!
> Oh, what a brick!
> Come here and kiss me quick!

Classy stuff, don't you think?

*Lucile has been watching this performance in stunned amaze-
ment and has still not yet recovered*

That's one of his best... But enough of this musical nonsense.
Here we've been, chatting away—chat, chat, chat—and I
haven't explained...

Lucile Explained what, monsieur?

Edouard Why I'm here.

Lucile (*with a little laugh*) I think I know that, monsieur!

Edouard You do?

Lucile Of course!

Edouard (*aside*) Dashed quick off the mark, these Parisian girls!

Lucile I was expecting you. And I'm fully prepared.

Edouard Are you? So you know a bit about me?

Lucile Only what I've been told. They say you're very fashion-
able.

Edouard My tailor's the best.

Lucile I mean in society.

Edouard Oh, rather! I know a prince, you know. To nod to.

Lucile When did you go to the Conservatory, monsieur?

Edouard The...? Well, I went this morning, in a manner of
speaking. But I don't feel the need now. In fact I never felt
better.

Lucile Am I right in thinking you won first prize?

Edouard First prize?

Lucile At the Conservatory.

Edouard The con—?Oh, the Conservatory! First prize at the
Conservatory. I see... Yes... No, I didn't. But I did once get a
prize for spelling. I was nine at the time. Hardly worth talking
about really; it was so long ago. Well, not all that long ago—
(*aside*) strange conversation!

Lucile (*aside*) He's very eccentric!

Edouard Yes... fifteen, sixteen years ago, to be precise. I was nine then; I'm twenty-five now, so that's...

Lucile (*surprised and delighted*) Twenty-five! That's a lovely age, monsieur.

Edouard (*fatuously*) Yes, it is, isn't it? It's a lovely sort of age to be...

Lucile (*collecting herself*) But for what we're here for today, age really doesn't matter a bit, does it?

Edouard Is that what you think?

Lucile Of course.

Edouard Ah. But you must admit the young have got what it takes.

Lucile On the other hand, the old have more experience.

Edouard More experience, maybe. But experience isn't everything. I know. From experience.

Lucile What does the proverb say? "If only age were able..." But then it goes on: "If only youth knew how..."

Edouard (*eagerly*) Oh, I know how, all right! I know how!

Lucile I'm sure you do, monsieur, but I didn't mean you. A man of your reputation doesn't need to prove his ability.

Edouard My reputation? God, what have they been saying?

Lucile I think it's more a question of me showing you what I can do, don't you think, monsieur?

Edouard You...? Me...?

Lucile Certainly.

Edouard (*delighted*) With pleasure! Whenever you like! Why not? Exactly what I came for! (*Aside*) I'm in paradise! (*He gets up and sits down in a state of frenzied excitement*)

Lucile is a little concerned

Lucile Are you quite well, monsieur?

Edouard Never felt better! I'm well; I'm happy; I'm rich!

Lucile Rich? Is that so?

Edouard Yes, terribly. I'm a millionaire, you know.

Lucile Ah! So it's purely for the love of the art that you're doing this.

Edouard Well, you could put it that way. The love of the art...of the art of love... And, of course, the love of the artiste!

Lucile (*curtseying*) Monsieur is too kind!

Edouard bows in acknowledgement. Both are entranced

Edouard (*coming back to earth*) What I mean to say, mademoiselle, is that as far as—how shall I put it?—financial considerations are concerned, I won't be at all difficult.

Lucile But, monsieur, I thought you knew what the arrangements were already.

Edouard Arrangements?

Lucile About the fees.

Edouard Fees! Nobody told me anything. (*Aside*) She's going to fleece me. I know she will.

Lucile Well, monsieur, it's four hundred francs a month for four sessions a week.

Edouard Sessions!

Lucile Of an hour each. Four per week.

A pause as Edouard takes this in

Edouard And all for four hundred francs?

Lucile You don't think it's enough?

Edouard (*aside*) And they said Paris was expensive!

Lucile Aren't you satisfied?

Edouard I'm astonished.

Lucile But, monsieur, you said you weren't going to be difficult... I'll tell you what, monsieur. If everything goes well, I don't see why we shouldn't think about a little bonus at the end of the month.

Edouard Oh, fine! Fine! I was going to mention a bonus myself. Yes, yes, yes... (*Aside*) So that's the catch. A little bonus!

Lucile It's settled, then. But really, you know, I shouldn't be discussing these details with you. If you really aren't satisfied with the terms you must talk to my mother about it.

Edouard Your mother?

Lucile Naturally, monsieur.

Edouard (*laughing*) Oh, your mother! That's a good one!

Lucile (*coolly*) Would you kindly explain the joke, monsieur?

Edouard You mean, mademoiselle, you actually have a mother? A real mother?

Lucile Of course! If it wasn't for my mother you wouldn't be here, would you?

Edouard Indeed no! (*Laughing*) And neither would you! (*Aside*) I'm not going to argue about it.

Lucile Do by all means discuss this affair with my mother.

Edouard Must I?

Lucile But I doubt if she will want the slightest alteration made to those conditions.

Edouard Oh, you mean the...

Lucile Four hundred francs a month for four sessions a week.

Edouard One hour per session.

Lucile Precisely. Agreed?

Edouard Oh, agreed! Agreed!

Lucile (*briskly*) Good! And now, if it's all the same to you, monsieur, I think we should make a start, don't you?

Edouard (*startled*) A start? What...? You mean... Just like that?

Lucile (*looking for something which she can't find; in the same brisk manner*) Why not? No time like the present, is there? That's odd. What on earth could I have done with it?

Edouard (*now also looking*) Are you looking for something, mademoiselle?

Lucile I must have left it in my bedroom. Will you excuse me, monsieur? I'll be with you again in a moment.

She goes into the bedroom

Edouard follows her eagerly but finds the door shut in his face. He thinks of going in after her, but decides against it. He walks away from the door, rubbing his hands with glee. He hears voices from the bedroom. He goes to the bedroom to listen

The door opens and Baptiste appears carrying a music stand and a score under her arm

She looks at him, he looks at her. He stands aside and lets her pass into the room. She puts down the music stand next to the piano and looks at him

Baptiste There you are, monsieur.

Edouard (*indicating the music stand*) What on earth is that?

Baptiste That, monsieur, is for this. (*She indicates the score which she places on the music stand*)

Edouard And what's that?

Baptiste That is mademoiselle's score, monsieur.

Edouard Is it? Ah. (*Intimidated, he strays towards the bedroom*)

Baptiste May I ask monsieur a question?

Edouard Yes. By all means.

Baptiste You haven't by any chance seen a young girl with a feather duster in here?

Edouard A feather duster? No. Why?

Baptiste I was expecting her. You see, it's my feather duster.

Edouard (*humouring her*) Ah. Well... If I see it, or her, I'll let you know. (*He edges towards the bedroom door*)

Baptiste May I ask if monsieur knows where he's going.

Edouard Yes, I do. That's the... That's where...
Baptiste Are you sure you know, monsieur?
Edouard Of course I'm sure. That's where mademoiselle sleeps.
Baptiste And Madame.
Edouard And who?
Baptiste Madame. Mademoiselle's mother.
Edouard You mean she sleeps with her mother?
Baptiste That's right, monsieur.
Edouard Good grief! Where do you sleep?
Baptiste I have a little room to myself, monsieur.
Edouard Let me get this quite clear——

Lucile enters carrying a rather long conductor's baton

Lucile Here we are! Found it at last.

Baptiste edges towards the front door

Where are you going, Baptiste?
Baptiste Mademoiselle——
Lucile Go and tidy up the bedroom.
Baptiste I've just been tidying it, mademoiselle.
Lucile Well, it's untidy again. Go along.

Baptiste goes to the bedroom

Edouard And be quick about it, Baptiste.

Baptiste exits to the bedroom

Lucile I beg your pardon, monsieur. Were you addressing my
maid?
Edouard Just telling her to hurry up in the bedroom. You know...
Lucile Why?

Edouard Well...

Lucile I think what goes on in my bedroom is my own affair, don't you, monsieur?

Edouard Yes... Yes, if you say so.

Lucile approaches Edouard with the baton. Edouard backs away

Lucile Here you are, monsieur.

Edouard My God, what is it?

Lucile I'm afraid it is rather a long one.

She hands it to him. He takes it gingerly

Edouard A long what?

Lucile It's your baton.

Edouard But what's it for?

Lucile I'm afraid I don't perform at all well without it.

Edouard You don't? How odd.

Lucile Please remember I'm only a beginner.

Edouard Surely not? (*Waving the baton vaguely*) Where shall I do...?

Lucile The beating, you mean?

Edouard Yes. If you really insist...

Lucile Do it on the music stand... No, it's too fragile... On this chair next to it.

Edouard Very well. Would you like it done... hard?

Lucile As hard as you like, monsieur. That's up to you. Shall we begin? (*She goes to the piano and sits down*)

Edouard Where are you going?

Lucile I'm going to start my piece.

Edouard But I thought you wanted me to beat...

Lucile That's right. On the chair.

Edouard You want me to beat the chair?

Lucile That's what I said, monsieur. (*Aside*) He can be rather dense at times. (*Pleasantly*) Shall we begin?

She settles herself to play her piece. Just as she is about to begin, Edouard starts vigorously beating the chair. It is heavily uphol- stered and as he beats it clouds of dust are emitted. Lucile looks up from her piano to stare at Edouard in amazement. Edouard meanwhile has been overcome by the dust. He abandons the beating and starts to cough violently

What's the matter, monsieur?

Edouard Dust!

Lucile But, monsieur, you're supposed to start beating after I've started playing. Aren't you?

Edouard Am I?

Lucile That's what always happened before.

Edouard Oh. Then that's what I'll do. (*Aside*) I'm out of my depth here.

Lucile (*pleasantly*) Shall we start again?

Edouard With pleasure.

Lucile begins to play — a simple piece and very badly — while Edouard starts to beat the chair vigorously, but quite out of time with the music. Lucile, naturally disconcerted by this, stops playing. Edouard continues to beat

Lucile Monsieur! Monsieur!

Edouard stops beating

Edouard Mademoiselle?

Lucile Excuse me, but I'm afraid I can't follow your beat.

Edouard You can't?

Lucile Could you make it more regular?

Edouard If that's what you want.

Lucile I don't think the piece requires that much rubato, do you?

Edouard (*baffled*) No. No. Hardly any.

Lucile So this time, more a tempo with the music.

Edouard Ah! You mean more in time with the music.

Lucile Yes, monsieur. (*Aside*) My mother's hired an idiot.

Edouard (*aside*) No wonder she charges so little. The girl's cracked.

Lucile (*pleasantly*) Shall we begin again, monsieur?

Edouard With pleasure, mademoiselle.

Lucile begins to play and Edouard beats time along with her. It goes rather well and they smile at each other. A rapport once more establishes itself. Lucile comes to the end of her piece but Edouard continues beating, as he does so coming nearer and nearer to Lucile

Lucile Monsieur! Monsieur!

Edouard Mademoiselle?

Lucile I've finished playing.

Edouard stops beating

Eouard Yes, of course. Do forgive me.

Lucile You got carried away, didn't you?

Edouard Yes, I did rather.

Lucile What shall we play now?

Edouard Well——

Lucile A little Beethoven perhaps?

Edouard Oh, no more music, please!

Lucile What!

Edouard Well, you play very nicely and all that, but wouldn't you rather do something else?

Lucile Not at all, monsieur.

Edouard I mean you can have too much of a good thing, can't you?

Lucile But I've only just started. Perhaps a little Mozart?

Edouard Mademoiselle, I don't wish to sound rude but, really, enough is enough.

Lucile But monsieur, please remember that we only have four sessions a week, each session lasting only——

Edouard One hour. Exactly. All the more reason to get on with it. If you're going to play the piano the whole time we won't get anything done, will we?

Lucile Won't get any what done, monsieur?

Edouard Well, any sort of... (*He laughs meaningly*)

Lucile (*aside*) He worries me.

She is about to start playing when Edouard, very masterfully, comes over and shuts the lid of the piano

Edouard Now then, enough of that! No more piano. You'll have plenty of time for that when I'm gone. (*Aside*) She's a terrible pianist anyway.

Lucile (*aside*) I don't understand his teaching methods at all.

Edouard Come! Sit over here.

He leads her over to the sofa and sits her down. He sits beside her

Now, let's chat. Dear mademoiselle—may I call you "dear", dear?—Do you like oysters? (*He takes hold of her hand*)

Lucile (*snatching it away*) Monsieur!

Edouard I ask you again—do you like oysters?

Lucile (*moving to the other end of the sofa from him*) Yes. Very much as a matter of fact.

Edouard Excellent! (*He takes out a notebook and writes in it*) Oysters, it is... And a bisque. What would you say to a nice bisque?

Lucile (*disturbed*) I don't think I've ever had one.

Edouard You'll love it, believe me. (*Writing*) Oysters and a bisque... Good! Now then, what else would you like?

Lucile Nothing... I don't know...

Edouard Fine! You leave it all to me. (*He writes some more in his notebook, then tears out the leaf and folds it up*)

Lucile (*aside*) At least he's harmless.

Edouard Do you have an envelope, mademoiselle?

Lucile On the table there, monsieur.

Edouard goes over and sits at the table

Edouard Are you doing anything at about midnight?

Lucile Me?

Edouard Yes. After the theatre tonight.

Lucile I'm not going to the theatre tonight.

Edouard I see! Your night off, is it? Splendid.

He devotes himself to addressing the envelope. She shakes her head despairingly. Then she watches him as he mutters to himself

Maxim's... Rue Royale... (*He takes a sheet of notepaper from the table and writes*) Please reserve private room... Midnight...

He turns to smile at Lucile who smiles back very nervously. He returns to his writing

Oysters... Bisque... Mmmhmm.

He turns back to Lucile who starts violently

Would you be so kind, my dear mademoiselle, as to ring for

your servant.

Lucile goes to the table at which he sits and picks up a small handbell

Lucile Certainly, monsieur. (*She rings it nervously*)

Baptiste appears immediately from the bedroom

Baptiste Mademoiselle rang?

Edouard My dear, would you have this sent by messenger at once. (*He hands her some money*) And keep the change, won't you?

Baptiste Very good, monsieur. (*She starts to exit* c *rapidly*)

Lucile Baptiste!

Baptiste Mademoiselle?

Lucile Don't go too far!

Baptiste No, mademoiselle.

She tries to indicate something to Lucile in sign language, but both Edouard and Lucile frown at her and she exits

Edouard So that's settled! Now what shall we talk about...? I know! Let's talk about your success. Do you know, I haven't seen the show yet?

Lucile What show?

Edouard You know! "Low-Life Lola" of course.

Lucile "Low-Life Lola"! Monsieur, I don't think that is a show for young ladies.

Edouard Ah, but I'm not a young lady, am I?

Lucile No, monsieur. That is not quite what I meant.

Edouard Anyway, I'm going as soon as I can get tickets.

Lucile Please do so, by all means, monsieur.

Edouard But only because of you!

Lucile Me!

Edouard Just you!

Lucile You're too kind. (*Aside*) Poor, poor boy!

Edouard After all, everyone is talking about you.

Lucile Me!

Edouard Just you! The idol of the men!

Lucile Oh!

Edouard The envy of the ladies!

Lucile Heavens!

Edouard And yet in spite of this fulsome praise you remain quite undazzled. At heart you are still a simple unaffected girl with a modest and tender heart. The glory has not gone to your head. Here you are, so charming, so welcoming in spite of it all. You put me at my ease instantly. Do you know something? When I first walked into this room—so chic—I was terrified. I trembled! And yet you didn't rebuff me. You welcomed me with your music... All that music... And instead of being thrown out on my ear, you did me the honour of accepting a little supper invitation at Maxim's. Mademoiselle, my dear, dear mademoiselle, permit me to tell you that you are an angel!

He begins to pursue her round the room, she retreating all the while

Lucile Enough, monsieur! Enough!

Edouard No, it is not enough! I am rich. I am a millionaire! I will give you everything you desire. Every whim of yours shall be satisfied. Four hundred francs a month, you say? Double that! Triple it! You shall have oysters for lunch, dinner, breakfast if you want them... If you want *me* a little... (*Seizing her hands*) Could you find it in your heart to want me, a little?

Lucile (*almost melting and then recollecting herself*) Please, monsieur! Unhand me!

Edouard Can't you feel it in your heart? The romance of love!
The romance of lovers through the ages. Romeo and Juliet...
Daphnis and Chloe... Abelard and Eloise... Well, there I was.
A Romeo without his Juliet. A Daphnis without his Chloe. An
Abelard without his... Well, never mind... And now I've found
them... her... you! It's you I love. And it's your love that has
driven me mad. Mad with passion! Mad, mad, mad!

Lucile (*shaking her head*) Mad!

Edouard (*trying to catch her*) Come to my arms!

Lucile Please, monsieur. Let go of me.

Edouard Did I frighten you?

Lucile Well, perhaps...

Edouard But, my dear mademoiselle, I wouldn't harm a hair of
your head. Don't tremble so, my dear, dear... Did my words
frighten you? Oh, my dear, everything I said was absolutely
rational.

Lucile Rational... Yes! (*Aside*) Never contradict a lunatic.

Edouard (*sitting on the sofa*) There! You see! I'm quite calm.
I'm sitting down. (*Patting a place beside him*) Come! Come!
Sit!

She sits on the sofa, as far from him as she can

There! We're not afraid any more, are we? Are we?

Lucile (*meekly*) No. But the things you said, monsieur...

Edouard Oh, come on... It isn't as if they haven't been said
before.

Lucile Monsieur!

Edouard Now then, don't be coy! It doesn't suit you.

Lucile I think there must be some misunderstanding, monsieur,
really——

Edouard But you do, like me, don't you? A little?

He takes her hand, she does not remove it

Lucile Well...
Edouard My angel (*He goes to kiss her*)
Lucile No... Please... Wait!
Edouard What?
Lucile My mother! She'll be here any moment!
Edouard (*laughing*) Your mother! That's a good one!

He takes her in his arms and kisses her. This time she does not resist

> *Suddenly the doors, c, open and Madame, Lucile's mother, enters, closely followed by Baptiste. Madame takes in the scene, outraged*

Madame Lucile!

Edouard and Lucile spring apart

Lucile Mother!
Edouard She's real!
Madame So this is what you do when my back is turned! (*To Edouard*) And who are you, monsieur?
Edouard I'm... I'm...
Lucile But mother, you know who this is. You hired him.
Madame I did what!
Edouard She what!
Lucile For four hundred francs a month, four sessions a month, an hour per session.
Madame I did not!
Edouard No, she didn't.

Madame (*to Edouard*) Be quiet, young man! Nobody asked you to interfere.

Lucile (*indicating Edouard*) Then he is not my piano teacher?

Edouard (*laughing*) Me! A piano teacher! That's a good one!

Madame Silence!

Lucile Then if he's not my piano teacher, who is he?

Edouard My name is Edouard Lorillot, and what I want to know is——

Madame Will you be quiet! (*To Lucile*) Do you mean to tell me, Lucile, that you were alone in this apartment, on the sofa, embracing a complete stranger?

Lucile But I didn't now he was a complete stranger, I thought he was a piano teacher, and that you knew him.

Madame This is no excuse. No excuse at all.

Edouard Now look here, Madame Dubarroy——

Madame For the last time, will you be silent! (*Slight pause. To Edouard*) I beg your pardon. What did you say?

Edouard I said "Now look here, Madame Dubarroy——"

Madame You called *me* Madame Dubarroy?

Edouard That's right.

Madame (*hitting him with her parasol*) How dare you!

Edouard You mean to say you're not Mademoiselle Dubarroy's mother?

Madame (*hitting him with her parasol*) How dare you?

Edouard (*to Lucile*) So you're not her daughter after all?

Madame (*hitting him even more violently with her parasol*) How dare you!

Edouard (*reeling under this last blow*) Then who in blazes is everybody?

Gabrielle enters with the feather duster

Gabrielle (*to Baptiste*) Thank you for lending me this. It came in very handy. (*She hands Baptiste the duster*)

Madame What is the meaning of this?

Baptiste (*responding to the signal; to Edouard*) Oh dear, monsieur, you must have come to the wrong appartment; if it's Mademoiselle Dubarroy you want, she's down below.

Edouard Eh?

Baptiste Oh dear, monsieur, you must have come to the wrong apartment; if it's Mademoiselle Dubarroy you want, she's down below.

Madame And very lucky she is to be there too! If I'd had my way she'd be in prison, for indecency!

Lucile (*to Edouard*) So you thought I was...

Edouard (*to Lucile*) Yes. I thought you were... And you thought I was... And you must have thought I was...

Madame So where is the maestro?

Everyone looks at her enquiringly

The music teacher.

Gabrielle Oh, him! He's downstairs with Mademoiselle Dubarroy. They met outside the front door. They're ever such old friends.

Madame Outrageous! (*To Gabrielle and Baptiste*) Come with me, both of you. I am going to sort this out once and for all!

She exits, followed by Baptiste and Gabrielle

A new shyness has fallen upon Edouard and Lucile

Edouard Mademoiselle...

Lucile Monsieur?

Edouard My name is Edouard.

Lucile Mine's Lucile.

Edouard (*bowing*) Enchanté, mademoiselle.

Lucile (*curtseying*) Enchantée, monsieur.

They smile and take a few tentative steps towards each other as the Lights fade or the CURTAIN *falls*

FURNITURE AND PROPERTY LIST

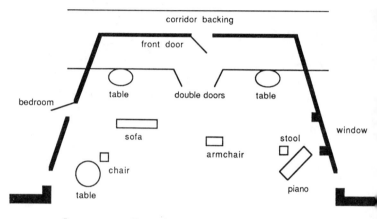

On stage: Round table. *On it*: envelopes and
writing paper, small handbell
Chairs
Sofa
Piano (either baby grand or upright)
Occasional tables with ornaments
Heavily upholstered dusty chair

Off stage: Music (**Lucile**)
Music stand and score (**Baptiste**)
Conductor's baton (**Lucile**)

Personal: **Baptiste**: feather duster
Edouard: visiting cards
Edouard: notebook and pen, money
Madame: parasol

LIGHTING PLOT

Property fittings required: nil
Interior. The same throughout

To open: General interior lighting

Cue 1 They step towards each other   (Page 31)
         The Lights fade

EFFECTS PLOT

Cue 1 **Lucile**: "... have to make." (Page 9)
Bell rings

Cue 2 **Baptiste**: "... or the maestro!" (Page 10)
Bell rings